To: Kazzie

From: Jonny

Copyright © 2005 by Blue Mountain Arts, Inc.

All rights reserved. No part of this publication may be reproduced, stored in a retrieval system or transmitted in any form or by any means, electronic, mechanical, photocopying, recording or otherwise, without the written permission of the publisher.

ISBN: 0-88396-971-8

Certain trademarks are used under license.

Manufactured in China.
First Printing: 2005

✺ This book is printed on recycled paper.

Blue Mountain Arts, Inc.
P.O. Box 4549, Boulder, Colorado 80306

THANK YOU

Blue Mountain Arts®
Boulder, Colorado

What Does "Thank You" Really Mean?

"Thank you" is one of those wonderful phrases people use to express a special gratitude. But there's often a lot more to it than those two words can say...

When it comes from
the heart,
from deep inside
the nicest feelings
and most special thoughts,
"thank you" means
so much.

It means thank you for taking the time to show that you care. It means "you really made my day," and sometimes it means you really make all the days so much better…

It means you make me feel so nice, and I wish I could do the same for you… just by letting you know how much you mean to me.

"Thank you" means you didn't have to...
but I'm so grateful you did.
"Thank you" means you've done something special that I'll never forget.

— Chris Gallatin

I Am So Grateful to Have You in My Life

It is not very often
we take the time
to show appreciation
for the people who mean
the most in our lives.
I want to tell you
how very much
you mean to me…

Sometimes in our
fast-paced days
so many things go unsaid
and so many people
get taken for granted.
I don't want that
to happen with us.

You are such an important person in my life —
one of the few people who cares so much and expects so little in return…

You go out of your way
to make my life happier,
and the little things you do
mean so very much to me.
You have such a big heart
filled with so much
kindness and love.

I feel so very lucky to
  know you
and I want to thank you
for all you do, all you are,
and for how wonderful
  my life is...
because you are a part
  of it.

— Elle Mastro

Let us be grateful to people who make us happy; they are the charming gardeners who make our souls blossom.

— Marcel Proust

I am so glad that you are here — it helps me to realize how beautiful my world is.

— Johann Wolfgang von Goethe

Thank You for Being So Nice

I am wondering if anyone
has taken the time to
thank you for being
 so nice...

You are a rare person
You are always so
 considerate of people —
putting their needs in front
 of yours

You are always so kind —
treating people in such a
caring way
If everyone were like you
the world would be
so peaceful...

Though people are often
  too busy
to stop and thank you
I hope you can feel
  the respect and love
that everyone has for you

And though many times
I have wanted to thank you
I never got around to it
So right now I want to
emphasize my thanks to you
for being such a
wonderful person

— Susan Polis Schutz

"Gratitude" is one of the nicest feelings a heart can have. It's a feeling that comes along for a very special reason — and it's a lovely thought that never goes away once it enters in.

Gratitude joins together with precious memories and grateful hopes. It lives on, not for just a moment or a day, but through all the seasons that lie ahead.

— Marin McKay

"Thank You" Just Doesn't Seem like Enough

Two words. Eight letters. "Thank you" just doesn't seem enough to express my gratitude for all you've done...

It doesn't seem enough to say, "What would I do without you?" It doesn't seem like enough for all you've given me. But that's the most amazing part… you give of yourself, expecting nothing in return.

I wish there were words to express how much I appreciate all you've done — how much I appreciate you. But there are no words, except two small ones that come directly from my heart… thank you!

— Donna Gephart

Your Kindness Will Never Be Forgotten

It's important that you receive the recognition and gratitude you so greatly deserve…

First of all, you're appreciated so much for what you've done. Second, it's comforting to know your heart is in it. Most of all, just knowing you are so thoughtful is a true gift in itself.

With your generosity, you lift spirits and make smiles appear. And now it's your turn to smile… Today, you're on the receiving end of the warmest thanks imaginable. Your kindness will always be remembered.

— Alicia Churchill

It is good to know you and to be touched by your kindness.
You have my warmest thanks.

— Paul Cézanne

Knowing that you are always here to understand and accept me helps me get along in the confused world. If every person could have someone just like you, the world would become a peaceful garden.

— Susan Polis Schutz

You've Made All the Difference

I've been through changes,
both good and bad,
and I've come to appreciate
the world's beautiful people
who keep alive
laughter, love, and hope…

You have a great gift,
and that gift is yourself.
I'd like to thank you
   for choosing
to share your gift with me.

Though no one person may be
able to change the world,
I want you to know
that you have made
a significant difference
in my life,
and I appreciate you.

— Grace F. Dement

A simple "thank you"
doesn't really measure up
to what I'd like
to say and give
for everything
you've given me.

I think, maybe a rainbow
or a jar of moonbeams
would be more appropriate.
I only wish I had them
to give to you.
Until then, I thank you
from the bottom of my heart.

— Debbie Avery Pirus

*You Work
So Hard
and Do
So Much*

Day in and day out, you make the world a better place to be. And the people who are lucky enough to be in your life get to see you're a very wonderful person with a truly gifted touch…

You go a million miles out of your way and you always do so much… to make sure that other lives are easier and filled with happiness. Your caring could never be taken for granted.

The people you're close to
are blessed… with someone
who works at a job well
done to bring smiles to the
day. You're a special person
who deserves more thanks
than this could ever say.

— Jenn Davids

*I Wish
I Could
Do This
for You...*

I wish I could make sure you always had the best — like laughter, rainbows, butterflies, and health. I wish I could take you anywhere you wanted to go and treat you to waterfalls, rivers, and mountaintops…

I wish I could guarantee you peace of mind, contentment, faith, and strength, as well as the constant ability to find joy in all the things that sometimes go unnoticed.

I wish you moments to connect with other individuals who are full of smiles and hugs to give away. I wish you could always know how much you are loved and appreciated.

— Barbara Cage

You're One of Those Rare People...

There are rare people
  in this world
who are so caring —
whose natural instinct is
to put someone else's needs
  ahead of their own...

There are rare people who
are always there to listen
with a smile and
a loving, open heart;
who never want or expect
praise for their good deeds
because that's just
the way they are.

You are one of
those rare people…

How fortunate I am
to have you in
my life!
— Andrea L. Hines

Thank you for being
a generous soul and
a beautiful spirit
in a world that
could use a million
more people just
like you.

Thanks so much for everything you've done and for all that you continue to do.
You're the best, and you're appreciated more than words can say.

— J. Kalispell

We wish to thank Susan Polis Schutz for permission to reprint the following poems that appear in this publication: "Thank You for Being So Nice." Copyright © 1989 by Stephen Schutz and Susan Polis Schutz. And for "Knowing that you are always…." Copyright © 1972 by Continental Publications. All rights reserved.